TOYS
Delights from the Past

by Ward Kimball

APPLIED ARTS PUBLISHERS

SECOND PRINTING   LEBANON, PA. 17042

Copyright 1976–Ward Kimball

ISBN 0-911410-40-6

Introduction

The earliest toys were handsome and quite limited in their variety. By the end of the 18th century, children were beginning to play with a small number of manufactured toys: hobby and stick horses, dolls, hoops, tops, balls, toy guns, swords and animal carts. With the beginning of the Industrial Age (early 1800's), commercially manufactured toys began to reflect the improvement of our living standards, along with the advances in technology and transportation.

By the 1860's, standardized toy designs began to be mass produced by the thousands in early factory assembly lines. In America and Europe a vast array of colorful and ingenious toys tempted youngsters to play with the delights of their Christmas dreams. New toys made of papier-mache, tin, wood and cast iron imitated in miniature the devices of the adult world. Little girls who aspired to be mothers or nurses now had a tremendous variety of dolls to choose from. Little boys who dreamed of becoming locomotive engineers or firefighters had a large choice of toy trains or horse-drawn fire engines to play with.

By 1900, competition among the many toy makers was intense. Hundreds of thousands of new American and imported toys filled the shops. The factories of Ives, Hubley, Arcade, Schoenhut, Marx, Straus, Lionel, Marklin, Bing, Doll, Planck, etc., were all part of a growing multi-million dollar world-wide business. The U.S. Patent Office recorded almost daily entries of new toy ideas. The introduction of home electricity soon made the electric train a household fixture. With the automobile came its miniature imitation. Every newfangled invention immediately had its toy counterpart. Inexpensive toys that ran, jumped, flipped, danced, marched, swung, climbed, chugged, squeaked, nodded, spun, whirled, boomed and banged, caught the fancies of the young as well as the old.

Let us now sit back and enjoy a few of these old toy delights and maybe smile a little as we remember.

U.S. Patent Office record of an improvement on Stevens & Brown Balancing Toy. Inventor's model, left and original toy, right.

TIN, WOOD and PAPER

◆ Our short photographic essay does not cover the early beginnings of toymaking when wood carvers, tinsmiths and other artisans made limited amounts of homemade playthings, but starts with a few toy examples turned out in the 1870—80's by the mechanized factories of New England and Europe.

Stevens & Brown tin "Mary's Little Lamb". (1870's)

Althof Bergmann tin Pie Wagon. (1870's)

Ives clockwork dancers. (1870's—1890's)

European "Jack-in-the-box". (1890's—1900's)

DOWN ON THE FARM

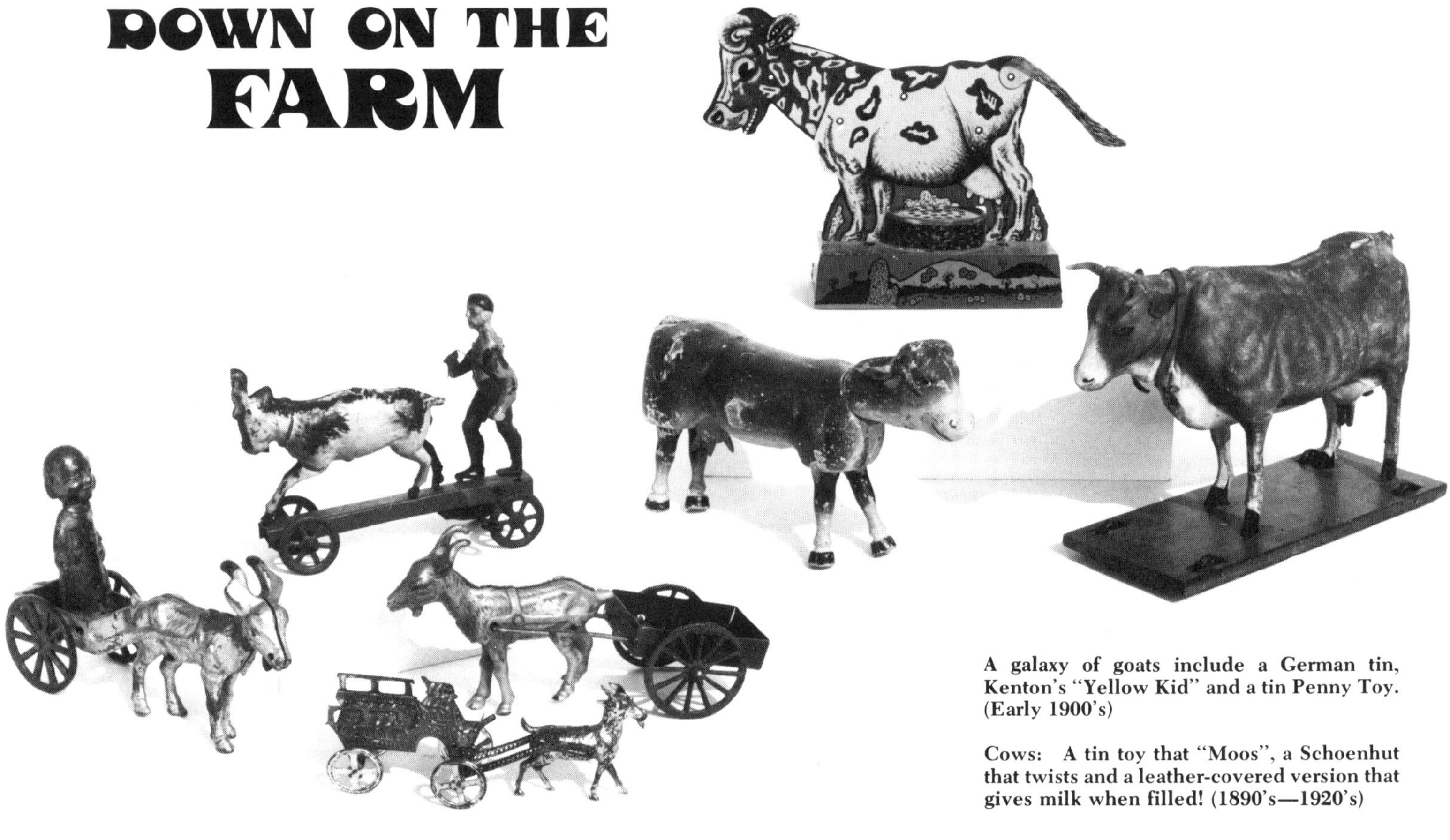

A galaxy of goats include a German tin, Kenton's "Yellow Kid" and a tin Penny Toy. (Early 1900's)

Cows: A tin toy that "Moos", a Schoenhut that twists and a leather-covered version that gives milk when filled! (1890's—1920's)

The Barnyard: A paper-covered Bliss Carriage Barn is surrounded by a display of farmyard accessories which include a Weeden steam tractor and examples of Hubley, Ideal and Kenton cast iron toys. (1900—1930's)

◆ We have always been a pet-loving people. The great number and variety of animal toys made for children attests to this. The most popular plaything was any toy featuring a horse. At one time, our society depended on the labors of the horse and his humorous spin-offs, the mules and donkeys. A farmer's cow also made good subject matter. Goat toys were much in demand as were mechanical or stuffed dogs. It remained for the lowly pig and the funny monkey to be the leading comedians in the toy parade.

A parcel of pigs: Mechanical walking pig, Paddy Bank by Ives, Lehmann "Paddy and Pig" and Schoenhut's wooden jointing pig. (1940, 1880's, 1900, 1905)

"Jennie, the Balking Mule"
by Ferdinand Strauss. (1920's—30's)

MAN'S BEST FRIEND: (clockwise from upper left.)
Musical clockwork poodle rises from hat, sticks out tongue. (1880's)
Stuffed cloth dog. (1900)
Borgfeldt "Pluto the Pup" (1930's)
Lindstrom Vibrating Dog. (1920's)
Schoenhut Poodle. (1905)
Somersaulting mechanical dog. (1920's)

DING-A-LINGS
(BELL TOYS)

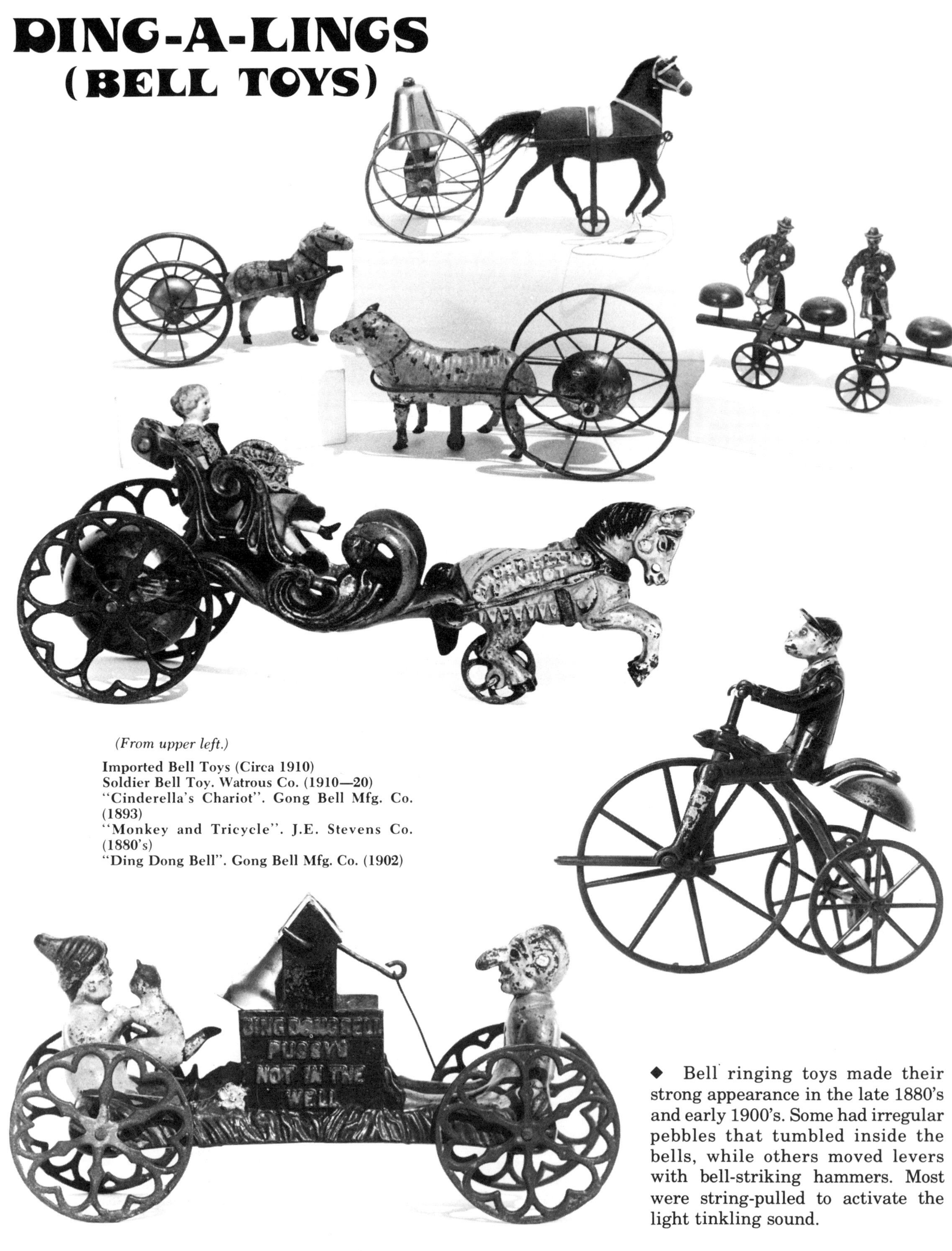

(From upper left.)

Imported Bell Toys (Circa 1910)
Soldier Bell Toy. Watrous Co. (1910—20)
''Cinderella's Chariot''. Gong Bell Mfg. Co. (1893)
''Monkey and Tricycle''. J.E. Stevens Co. (1880's)
''Ding Dong Bell''. Gong Bell Mfg. Co. (1902)

◆ Bell ringing toys made their strong appearance in the late 1880's and early 1900's. Some had irregular pebbles that tumbled inside the bells, while others moved levers with bell-striking hammers. Most were string-pulled to activate the light tinkling sound.

SHIP AHOY!

◆ Nautical toys were not always designed with water in mind. There were alcohol-burning steamers and clockwork-propelled boats, but the majority of toy boats "sailed" on wheels and were made of paper, wood or even cast iron!

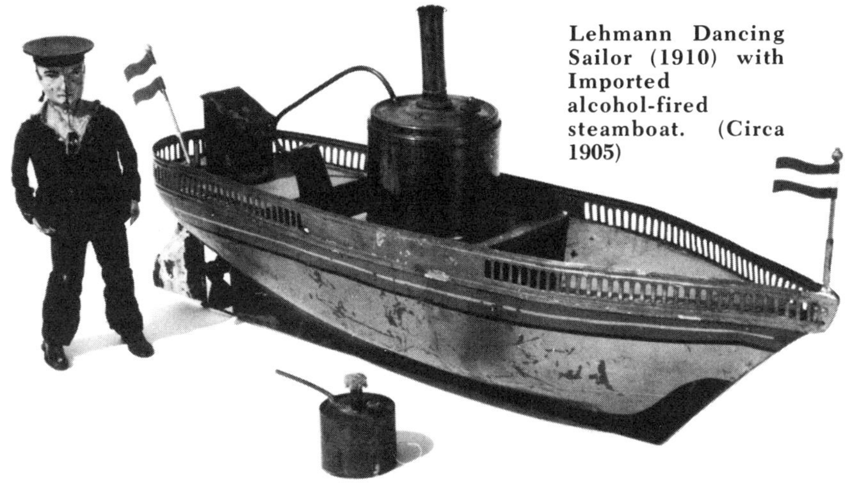

Lehmann Dancing Sailor (1910) with Imported alcohol-fired steamboat. (Circa 1905)

Cast iron riverboats by Harris (1903), Dent (1900)

U.S. Hardware Co., cast iron Rowing Scull. (1898)

Wood and paper boat. Can be dis-assembled with parts stored in hull. (1880's)

GREATEST SHOW ON EARTH

◆ The once-a-year thrill of a circus coming to town used to be the biggest thing in a kid's life. The rest of the time he could relive that exciting event with a generous assortment of circus toys. The Hubley Company's famous cast iron "Royal Circus" parade of wagons was unmatched for color and realism. Schoenhut's circus featured a real cloth tent to be filled with an amazing array of animals and human performers that could be joined together in an endless variety of death-defying poses. The last of the toy circus offerings was Lionel's Mickey Mouse circus of 1936, complete with train and cardboard tent displaying cut-out cartoon characters.

Schoenhut Acrobats. (1905)
Hubley cast iron Royal Circus Wagon. (1920's)
Circus Picture Books, left. (1888)
Marx "Ring-A-Ling" Circus. (1920's)
Hubley cast iron Circus Band Wagon. (1920's)

Schoenhut adjustable circus clowns. (circa 1905)

Ives Walking Bear contemplates
European tin brother. (1880 and 1903)

Schoenhut Circus Lion
and Leopard fight over
fallen Ringmaster.

Martin's "Mysterious Ball"
spirals upward to open and
display man at top.
French, 1906)

Strauss Auto Cage Wagon with articulated
ring master and lion (1920's)

TOYS
Delights from the Past
9

MEN WORKING

◆ Toys that imitated the trappings of business trades or the great machines of industry were a natural result of our technological expansion. They were a constant though questionable reminder to youngsters of the value of hard work. Conversely, with the Great Depression, many amusing toys reflected the carefree life of the tramp or hobo whose only nemesis seemed to be the barking dog or the pursuing cop!

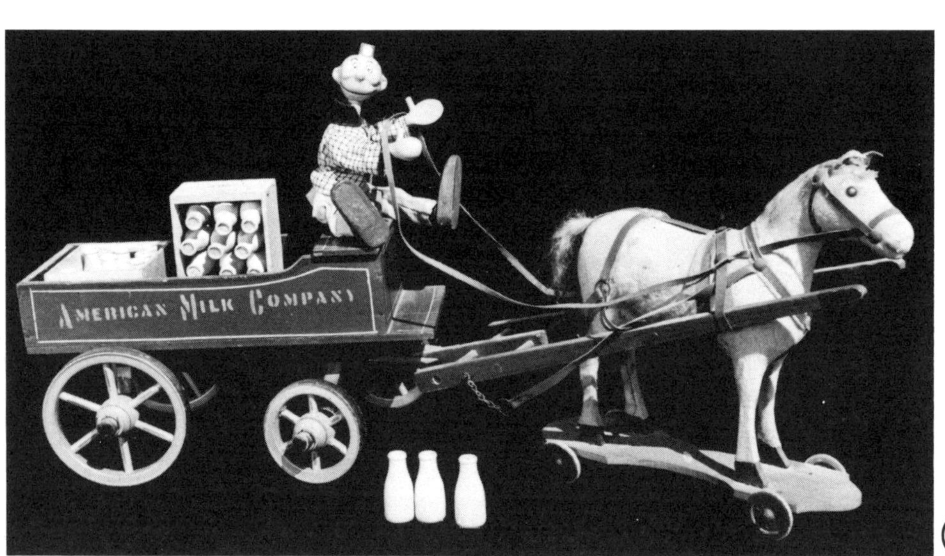

...and NOT WORKING

(1) Bing Steam Engine (1920) with factory workers. (1902)
(2) Schoenhut "Happy Hooligan" (1924) and Milk wagon. (1910)
(3) "Panama Pile Driver". Marble power raises and lowers tram. (Circa 1920)
(4) Marx "B.O. Plenty", Dick Tracy's friend. (1940)
(5) Unique Mfg. Co. "Hobo Train" with animated characters. (1930's)
(6) Schuco "Charlie Chaplin" waddles with whirling cane. (1920's)

"Sunny Andy-Fun Fair" is actuated by gravity propelled marbles. Behind are various teeter and swing toys.

◆ Real life teeter-totters, swings, Ferris wheels and merry-go-rounds all had toys to match. Some of these toys were activated by gravity, some with spring motors and a few by heavy steel marbles. They all featured happy kids enjoying themselves.

Ferris Wheel and Merry-Go-Round. Both toys are spring-wound and are musical. (European, Circa 1905)

TOYS
Delights from the Past

MAIN STREET, U.S.A.

◆   Wheel toys have always led the playtime parade, especially in the days of the horse. Carriages and wagons of every description had well-sculptured horses that appeared to be trotting, prancing or galloping. Then came the automobile. This important event provided a whole new succession of horseless carriage toys. The spring-wound motor became the ideal source of propulsion for the many trips down the sidewalk or across the kitchen floor.

Wilkins cast iron
Horse Car. (1890's)

DING! Goes the TROLLEY
...and the HORSE CAR

◆ Before the luxury of home electricity, the tin, wood and cast iron toy horsecars were motivated by pushing or pulling with "string power." But in the early 1900's, toy firms like Carlisle & Finch, Howard, Voltamp and Lionel changed all this with the ultimate in realism: electrically propelled trolleys! The earliest versions, like the Lionel below, were powered by wet or dry cell batteries.

Voltamp 2″gauge Electric Interurban. (1911)

Lionel 2 ⅞″ gauge Electric
Trolley. (1901—1905)

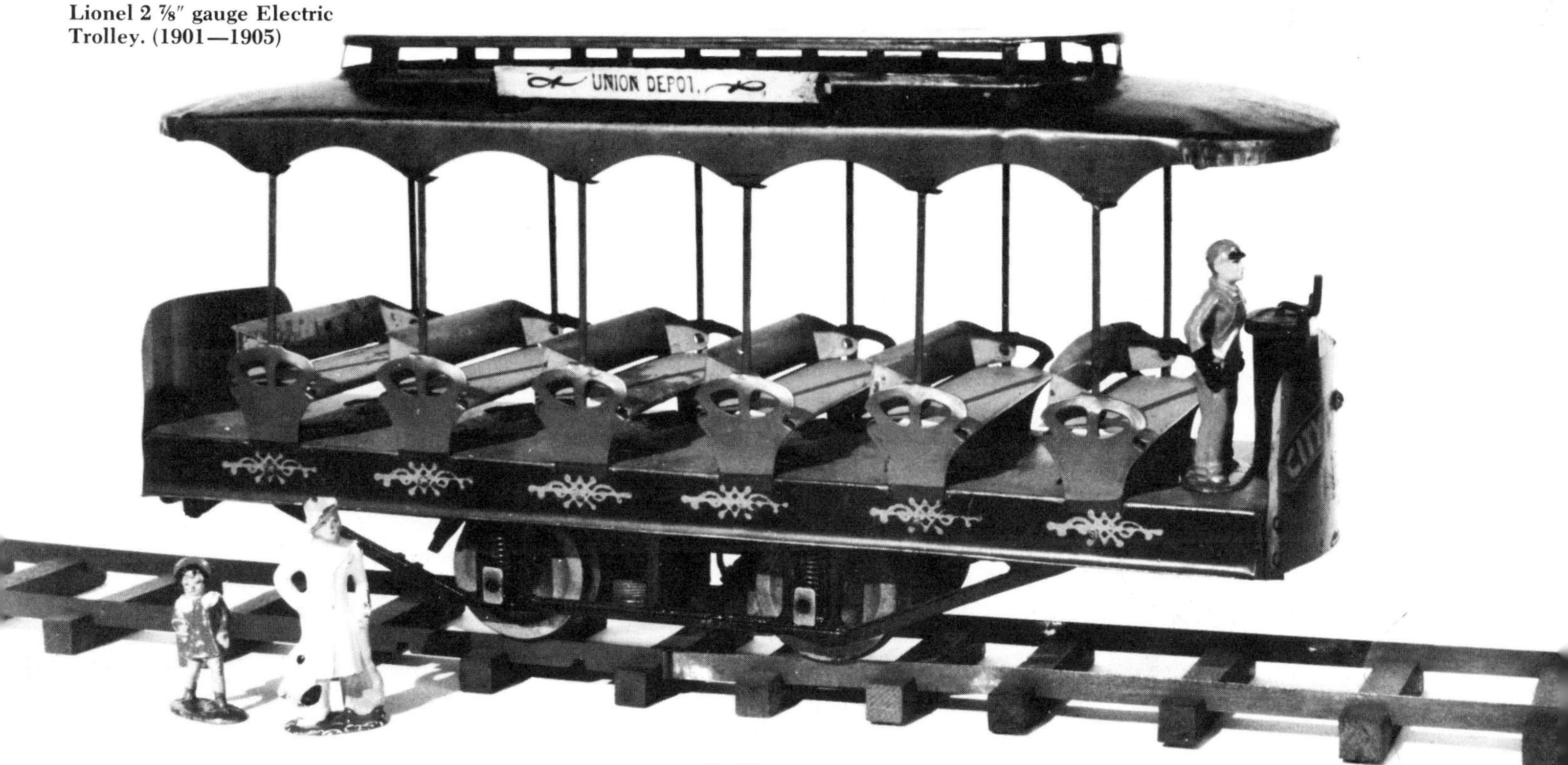

TOYS
Delights from the Past
13

GET a HORSE!

. . . or an OX
. . . or a MULE
. . . or a DONKEY

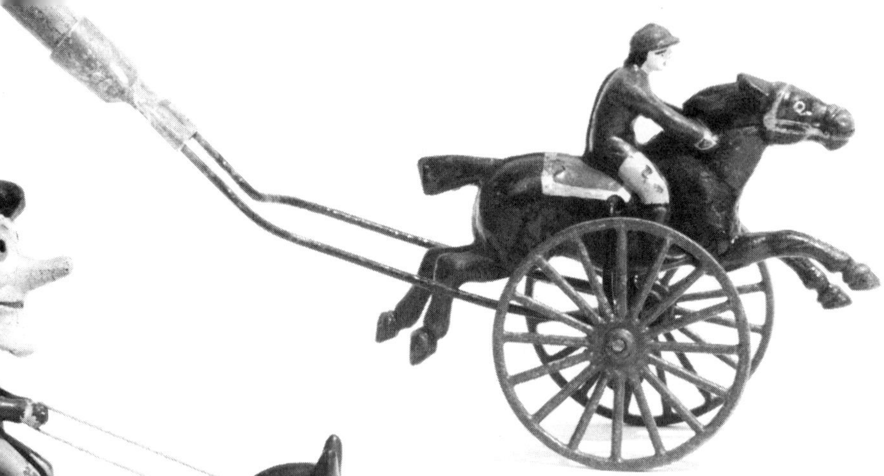

Wilkins cast iron Jockey and Horse. (1900—1912)

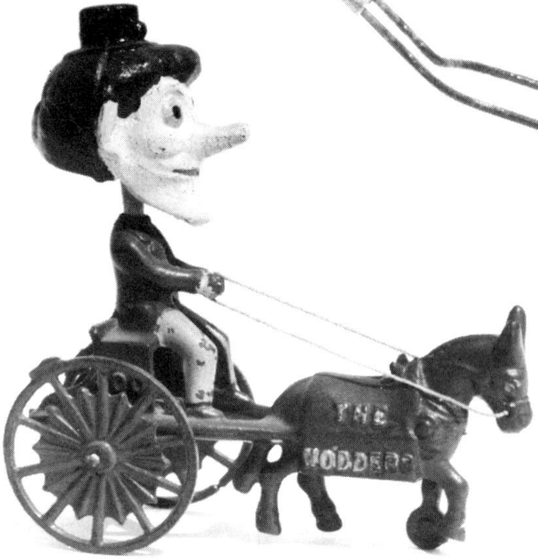

Hubley cast iron "Nodder", (1910)

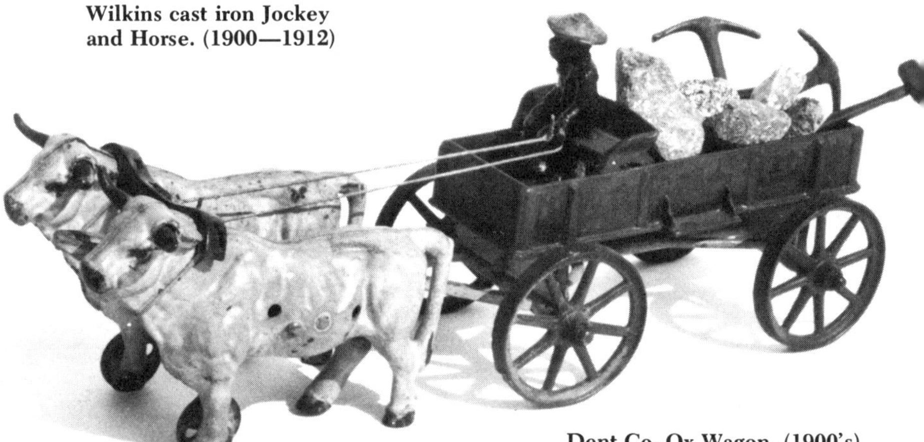

Dent Co. Ox Wagon. (1900's)

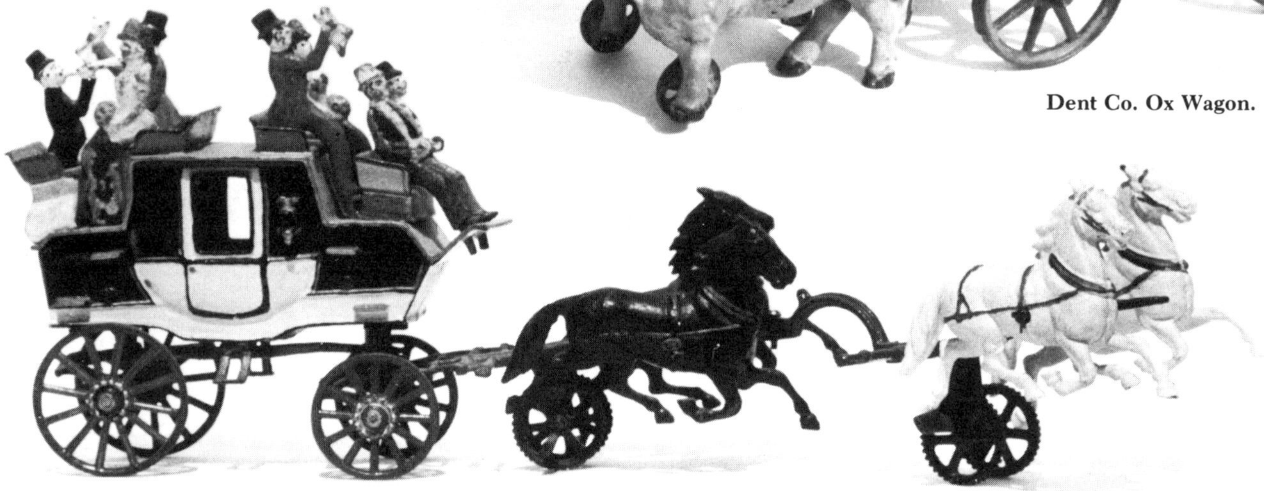

Carpenter cast iron "Tally-Ho". (1880's—90's)

Hubley cast iron Ice Wagon. (Circa 1910)

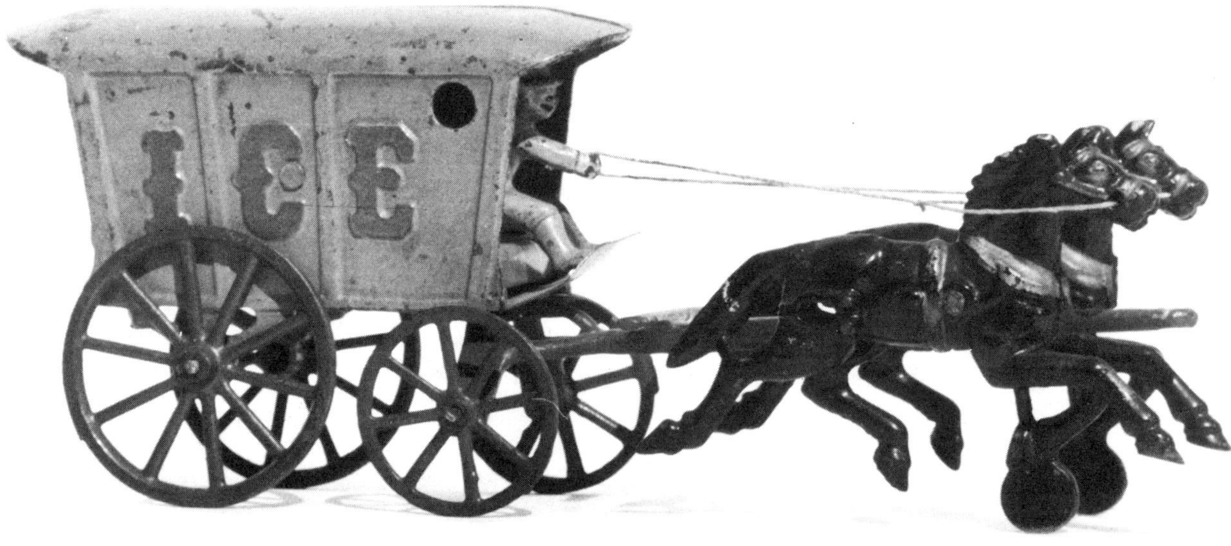

◆ Sometimes it's hard to believe that our daily lives once depended so heavily on beasts of burden. Naturally, the toy conveyances of that period were pulled mostly by horses, sometimes by mules or donkeys, occasionally by oxen, and even by goats.

Wilkins cast iron
Beer Wagon. (1910)

Kenton cast iron
Log Wagon. (Early 1900's)

Wilkins cast iron
Pony Cart. (Early 1900's)

Wilkins cast iron
"Boy's Express" wagon.
(Early 1900's)

WORKING on the RAILROAD

◆ Next to the doll, probably no plaything in the long history of toys has enjoyed the popularity or has been made in such quantity as the toy train. From Francis Field & Francis in the 1840's down to Lionel in the 1970's, toy trains of every color, size and description have delighted children of ALL ages. Because of its design and size, the train was usually packed away to be used only at Christmas. That is probably why so many well-preserved examples are still being discovered. The earliest designs were either pulled, powered by clockwork, or propelled by steam. With the introduction of electricity, the toy train reached a new peak of popularity which it still enjoys.

Knapp Locomotive #222 in grade crossing mishap with Bing Model T Ford. (1905 and 1920's)

Fallows Co. trackless tin train. (1883)

Jean Schoenner alcohol-fired steam locomotive and train (1880—1890)

Milton Bradley wood and paper trackless floor train. (1890's)

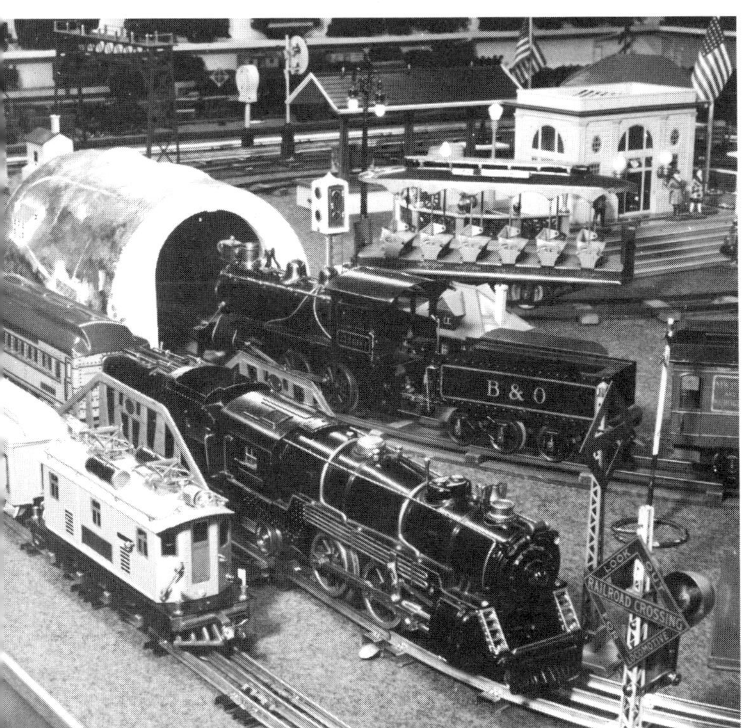

Lionel 'O' gauge #256, American Flyer standard gauge #4670, Voltamp 2″ gauge #2100 and Lionel 2⅞″ gauge trolley. (1901-1930)

Distler Co. European circle R.R. (1920's)

Carpenter cast iron locomotive. (1880's)

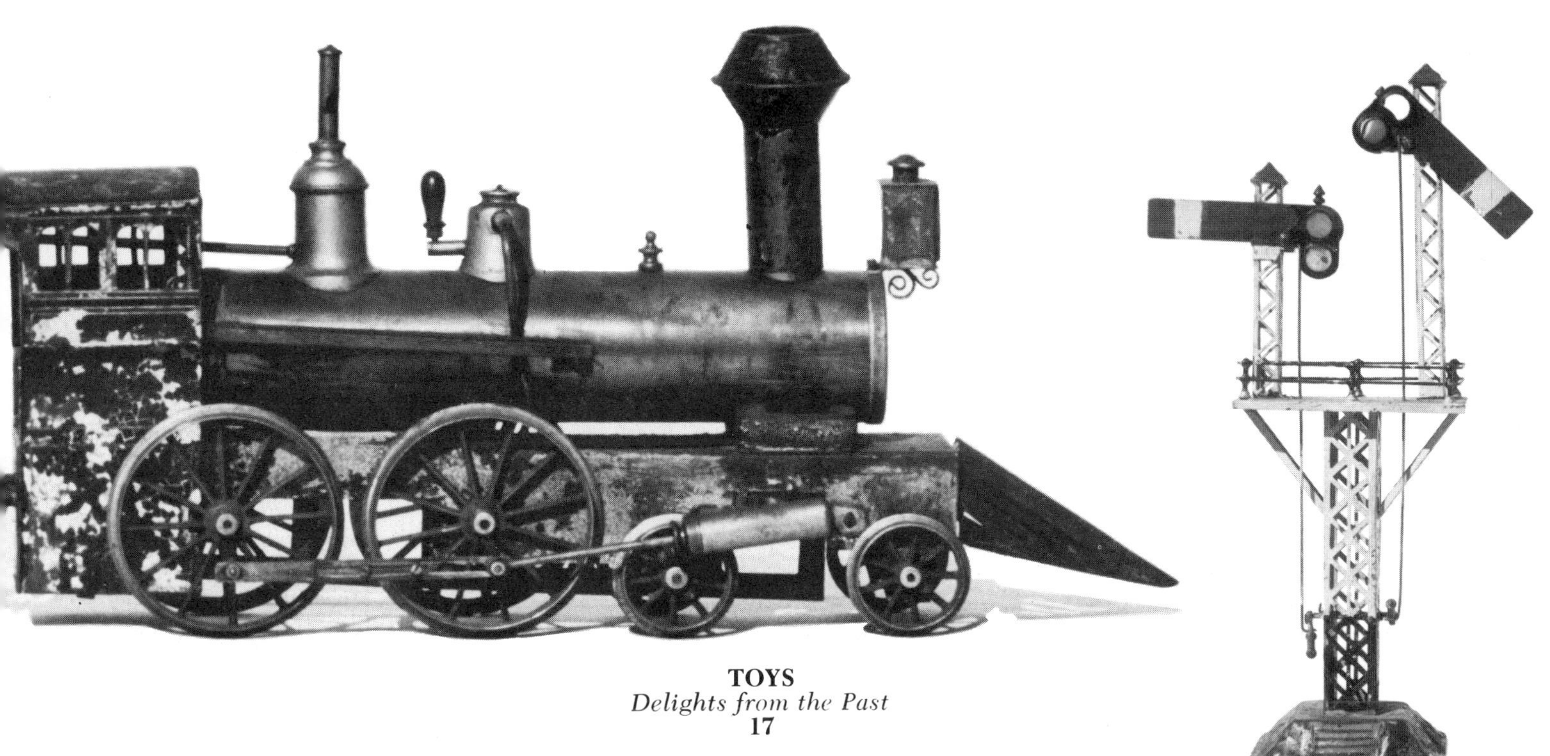

TOYS
Delights from the Past
17

BIRDS and the BEES

◆ No object or living thing escaped the exploitation of the toy designer. Toy birds whimsically pulled carts, flapped their wings and laid eggs. They managed to do everything but fly!

Lehmann Ostrich Cart (1890) tops a variety of tin and wood mechanical fowl.

◆ The varmints too, have always been represented in the toy menagerie: everything from tin lady bugs to cast iron grasshoppers and even frogs that actually croaked.

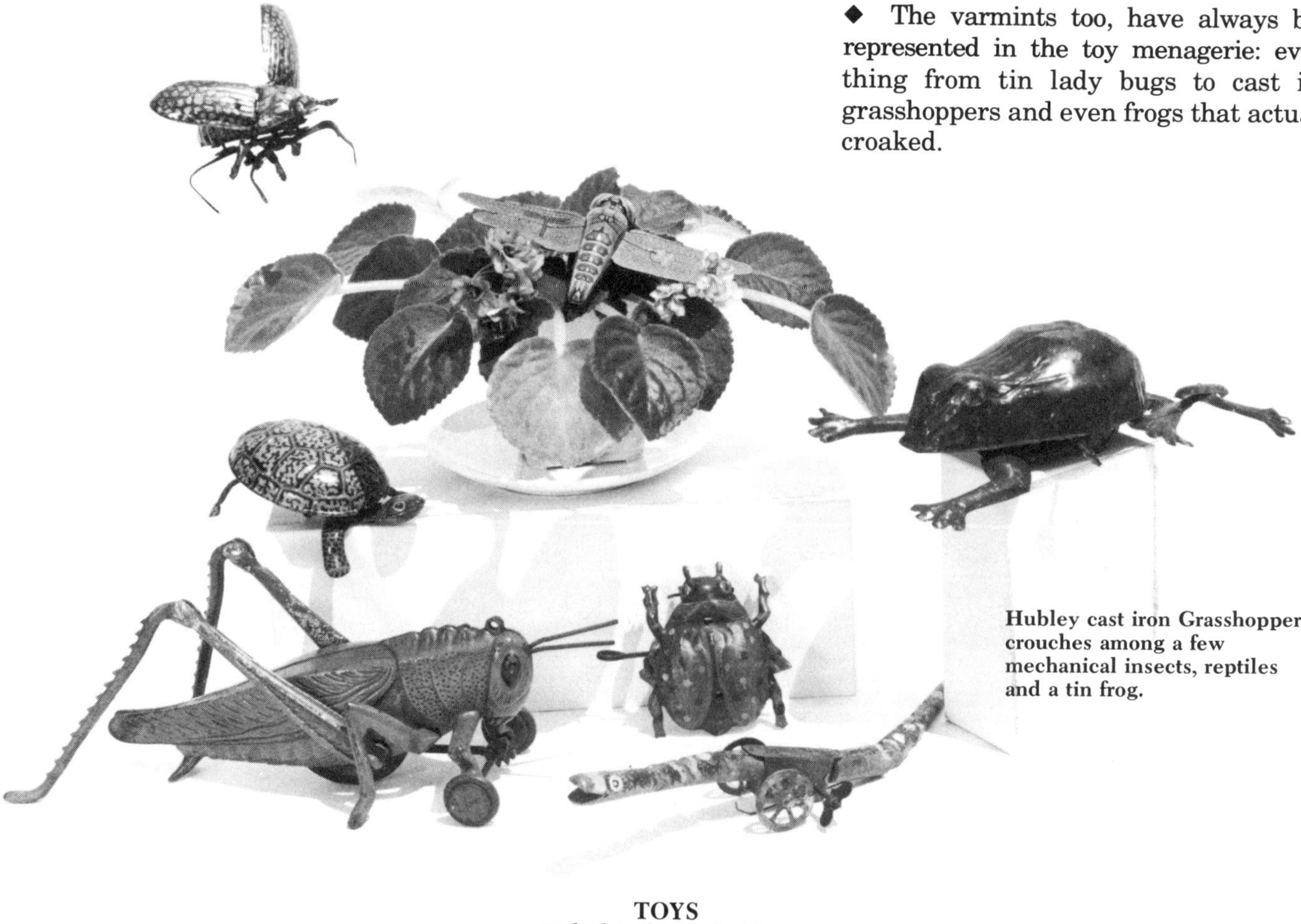

Hubley cast iron Grasshopper (1920's), crouches among a few mechanical insects, reptiles and a tin frog.

SUGAR and SPICE

◆ No toy compendium, however limited, should be without tribute to the doll, historically the most popular of all toys.

"Mary's Little Lamb".
Cloth, wood and paper.
(Imported, 1880's)

Jumeau Walking Doll. (France, circa 1890)

TOYS
Delights from the Past
19

Horse and Wagon toy with doll. (U.S. circa, 1905)

Ives cast iron Artillery Carriage. (1880's—90's)

SOUND THE BUGLE!

◆ Since the beginning, the toy soldier has never seemed to lose his appeal. In times past, childhood indoctrination to the military sometimes began with a sword, a toy pistol, or a regiment of highly decorated soldiers presented as a birthday or Christmas gift. Even today, toy soldier buffs, young or old, fight the famous battles of history on the plains of the dining room table.

Barclay and Manoil Co. cast soldiers in battlefield array. (1930—40)

Teddy Roosevelt leads charge of cardboard Rough-Riders. (1900)

◆ The similar utility of real life motorcycles and horses is also quite obvious in their toy counterparts. Here, as in other toys, designs came in tin, wood and cast iron to roll, spin, buck or jump.

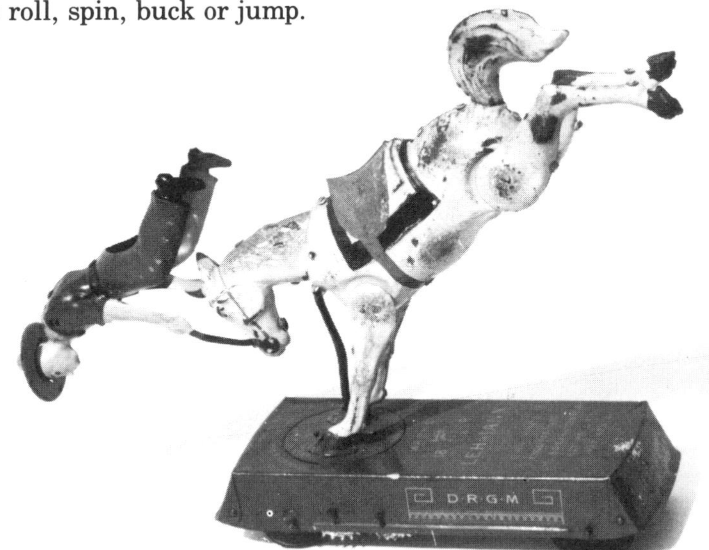

(From top left.)
Lehmann and German spring-wound motorcycles. (1920's)
Hubley cast iron "Traffic Car". (1930's)
Hubley cast iron Side Car Cycle. (1930's)
Lehmann tin "Bucking Bronco". (1907—1924)
European tin cowboy. (Circa 1910)
Unique Art Co. "Rodeo Joe" funny car. (1940's)

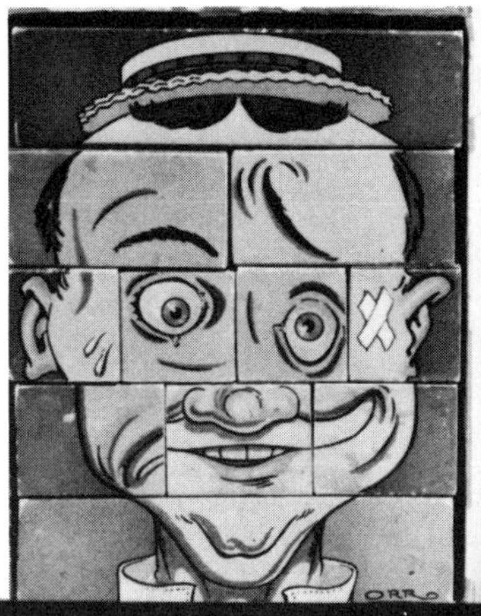

The Many Faces of Toys

◆ The naïve whimsy and primitive folk art quality achieved in so many of the old toy figures culminated in the expression and rendition of the faces. The many unknown craftsmen who hand-painted or designed these visages are long gone, but their work lives on to amuse and amaze.

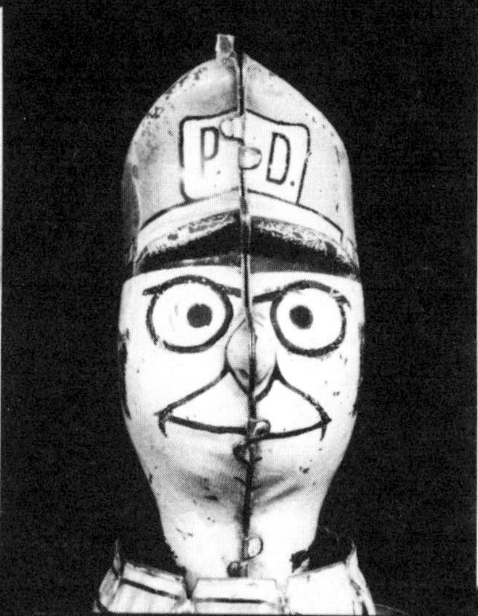

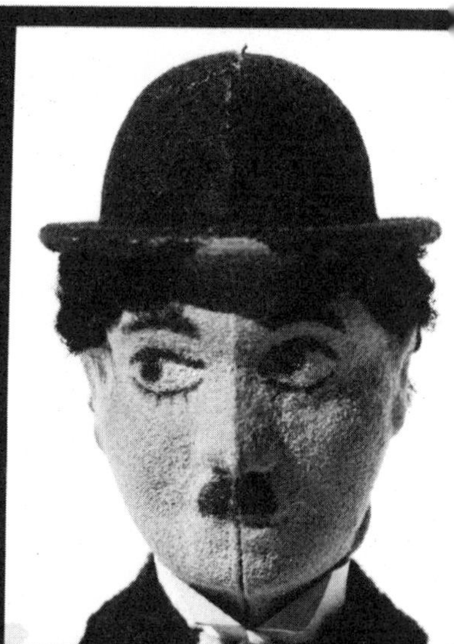

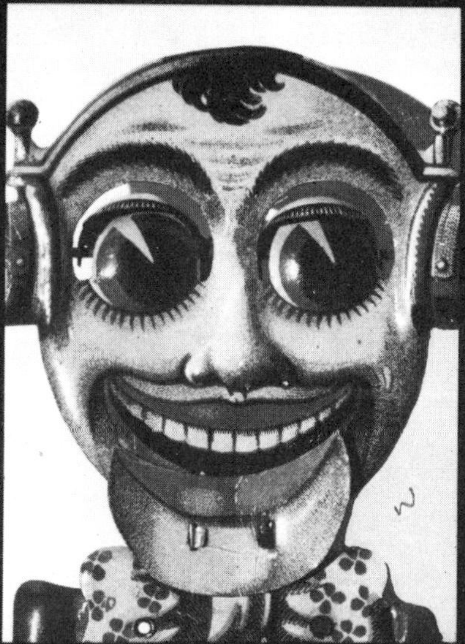

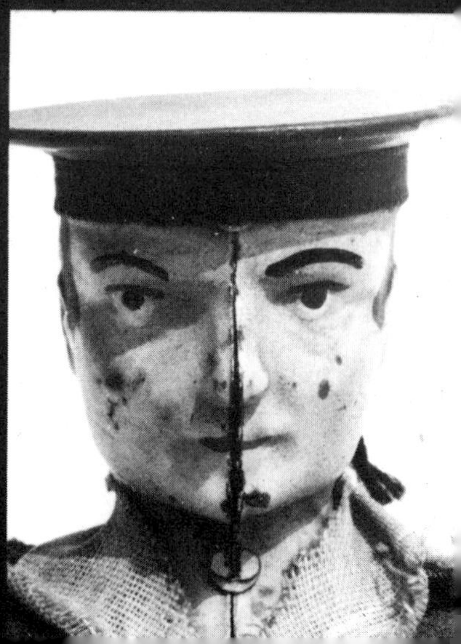

Let There Be MUSIC

Marx "Merriemakers" mouse band. (1930)

Mechanical Musicians serenade revolving dancers. (Tin, early 1900's)

◆ They dance, play, plunk and jig. These are the old fun toys. When the springs are wound to start them bouncing and clattering, they never cease to evoke a smile or even an outright guffaw.

Strauss "Ham and Sam". (1920's)

Marx "Charleston Trio". (1920's)

Unique Art Co. "Jazzbo Jim". (1920's)

Lehmann "Alabama Jigger". (1904—1914)

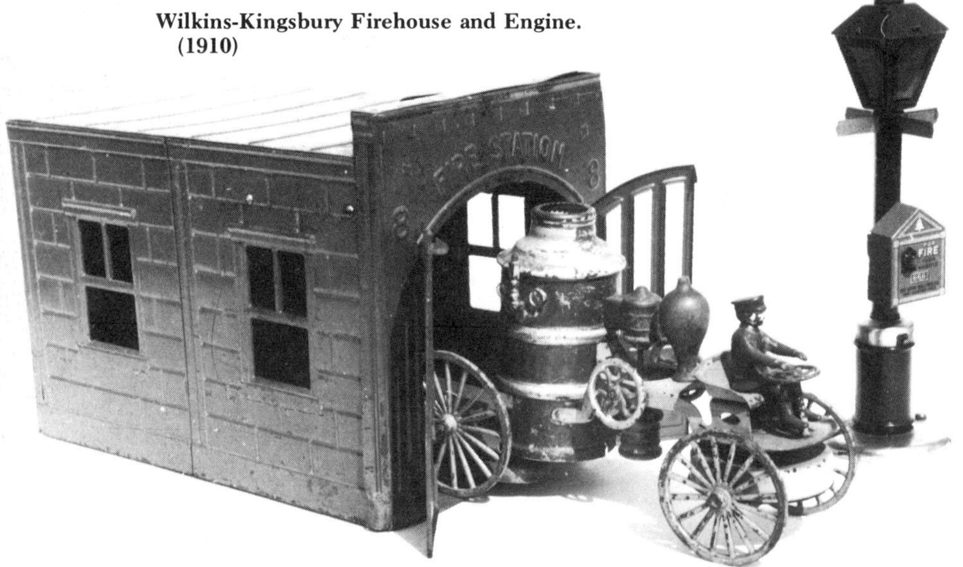

Wilkins-Kingsbury Firehouse and Engine.
(1910)

FIRE!

◆   Most every toy factory had its stable of fire toys. Next to being a locomotive engineer, a boy likely dreamed of becoming a fireman. Toy makers accommodated this fantasy by turning out complete fire departments in the multi-thousands. Pictures of horse-drawn firechief wagons, steam pumpers, hook & ladders and patrol wagons, even bell-ringing firehouses filled the old toy catalogues. Later, toy fire equipment became motorized to keep up with the times.

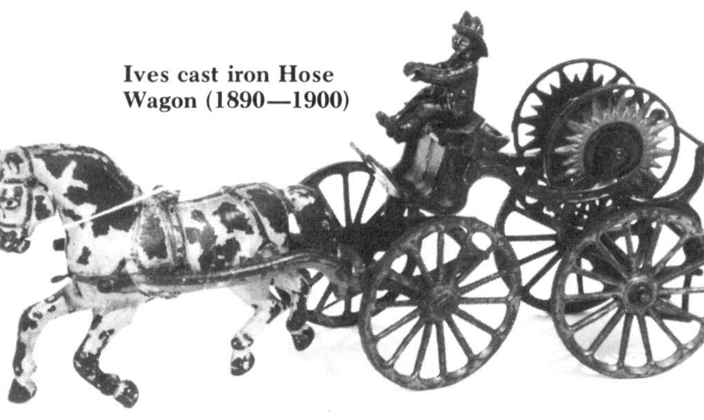

Ives cast iron Hose
Wagon (1890—1900)

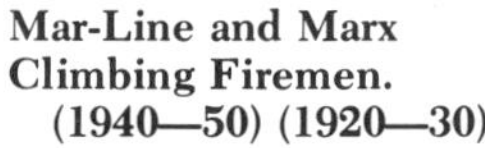

Hubley cast iron
Ladder Truck (1920—1930)

Kenton Hook and Ladder (1890's). Dent Fire Engine (1900)

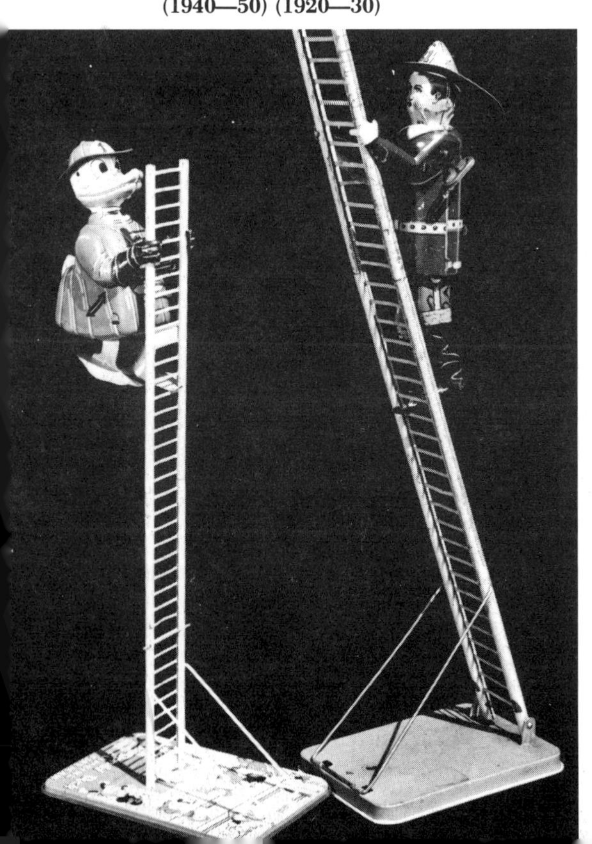

Mar-Line and Marx
Climbing Firemen.
(1940—50) (1920—30)

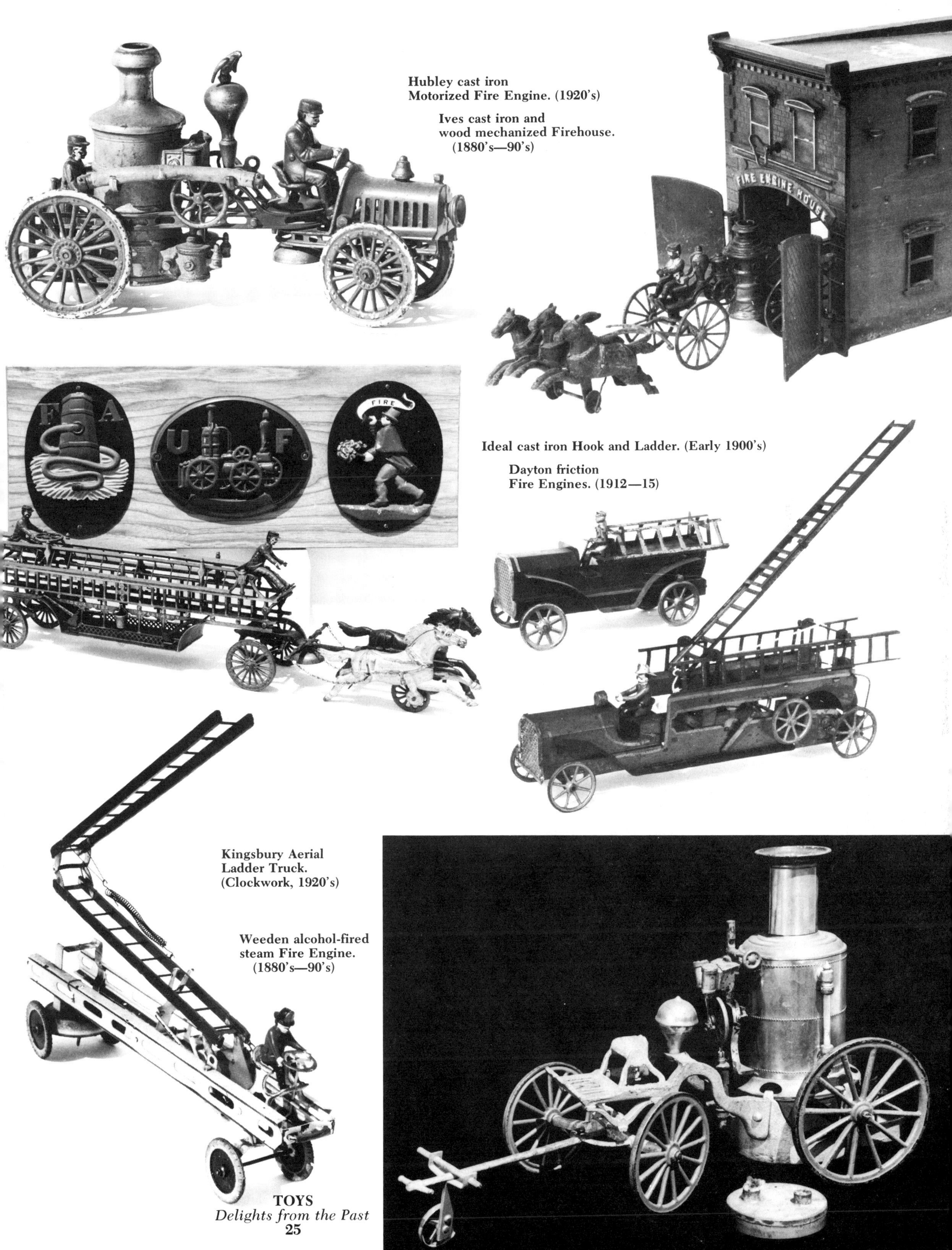

Hubley cast iron
Motorized Fire Engine. (1920's)

Ives cast iron and
wood mechanized Firehouse.
(1880's—90's)

Ideal cast iron Hook and Ladder. (Early 1900's)

Dayton friction
Fire Engines. (1912—15)

Kingsbury Aerial
Ladder Truck.
(Clockwork, 1920's)

Weeden alcohol-fired
steam Fire Engine.
(1880's—90's)

TOYS
Delights from the Past
25

EASTER PARADE

European embossed cardboard and wood. (1890's)

◆ Along with Christmas and birthdays, Easter was a time to receive toys. Rabbits, chicks and eggs made excellent themes for imaginative toy designs.

Nifty metal pull-toy. Bunny lifts shell as chick pecks. (1920's)

Lionel Peter Rabbit mechanical handcar. (1936)

No Place Like Home

Bliss wood and paper Doll House and Santa toy. (1900—1905)

◆ So long as there are dolls to play with, there will be doll houses to fill with miniature furnishings. Most of these structures were handmade, one-of-a-kind, but a few companies like Bliss manufactured a full line of detailed, lithographed, paper-on-wood abodes, trimmed with generous amounts of architectural gingerbread.

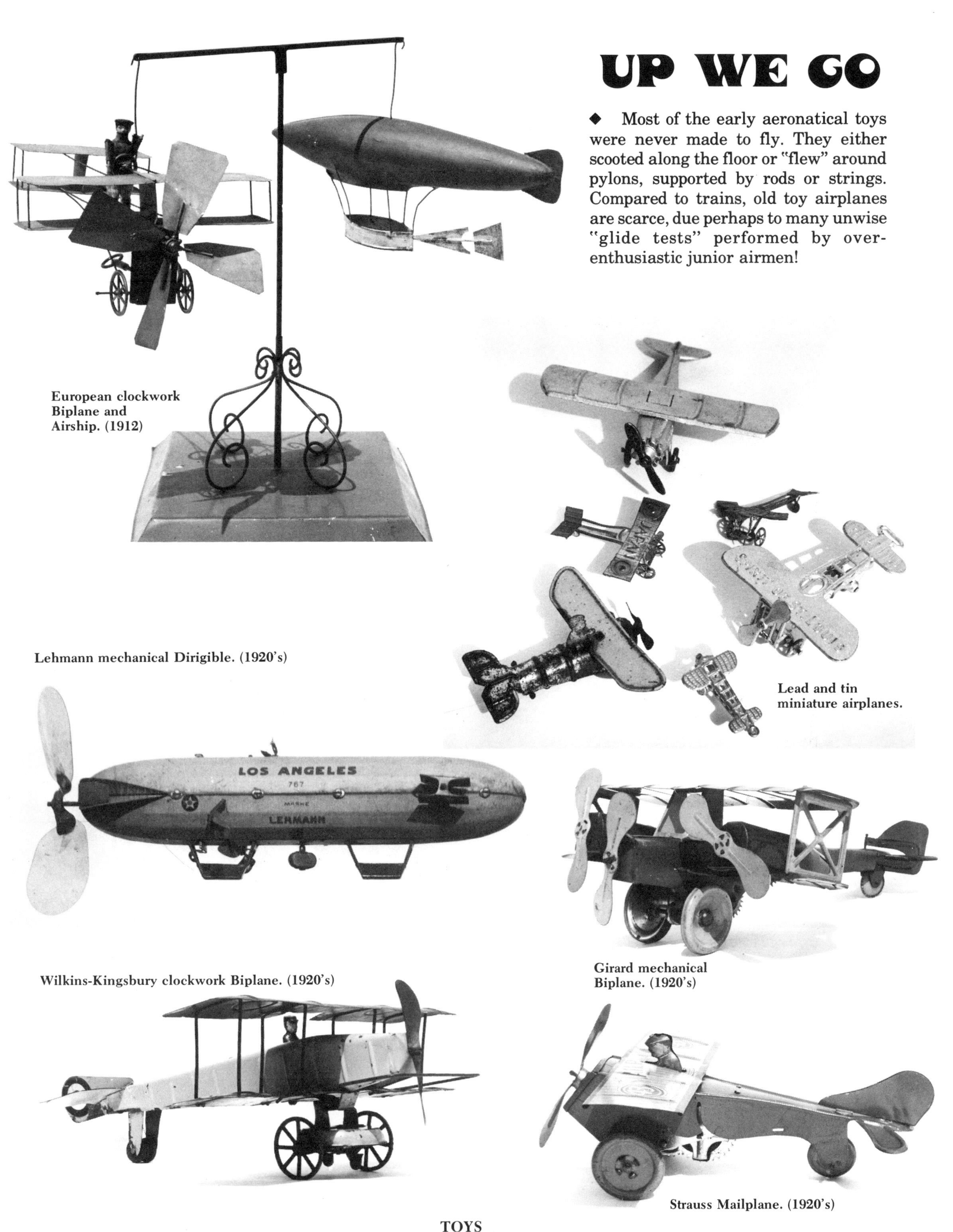

UP WE GO

◆ Most of the early aeronatical toys were never made to fly. They either scooted along the floor or "flew" around pylons, supported by rods or strings. Compared to trains, old toy airplanes are scarce, due perhaps to many unwise "glide tests" performed by over-enthusiastic junior airmen!

European clockwork Biplane and Airship. (1912)

Lehmann mechanical Dirigible. (1920's)

Lead and tin miniature airplanes.

Wilkins-Kingsbury clockwork Biplane. (1920's)

Girard mechanical Biplane. (1920's)

Strauss Mailplane. (1920's)

"SEE YOU IN THE FUNNIES"

◆ At an early age we learn to ferret out the best part of the fat Sunday newspaper: the funny pages. During the 1920's and 30's, toy makers were quick to capitalize on this young hero worship of our favorite comic strip characters and turned out an amazing line of comic toys now so esteemed by young collectors. Mickey Mouse led the volume parade to be challenged only by Peanuts' "Snoopy" in today's market.

1. Happy Hooligan by Chein and Schoenhut. (1932 and 1924)
2. Felix the Cat adjustable doll. (Circa 1925)
3. Popeye the Sailor by Marx, Chein, Mar-Line. (1930—40—60)
4. Disney Toys. Mar-Line. (1950's—60's)
5. Charlie McCarthy by Marx. (1939)

6. Mickey and Minnie Mouse puppets. (1930)
7. Barney Google and Spark Plug by Nifty. (1924)
8. Toonerville Trolley by Nifty, Kempton and Dent. (1922—39)
9. Andy Gump by Arcade. (1924). Tootsietoy. (1932)
10. Mutt and Jeff. Swiss. (1940's)

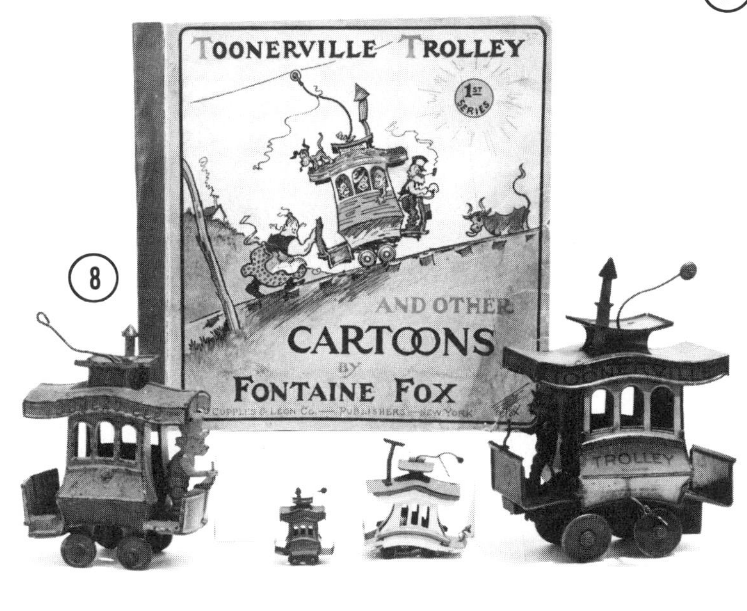

Bing clockwork auto with Arcade cast iron signs.

The Horseless Carriage

◆ In toyland also, the introduction of toy automobiles around 1900 signalled the demise of horses used for pulling transportation toys. These model cars heralded the new age and every kid just had to own one or two, and maybe more if he collected the mini "Tootsietoys."

Strauss mechanical bus. (1920's—30's)

Harris cast iron mechanical auto. (1903)

Lehmann automotive toys. (1907—1925)

TOYS
Delights from the Past
30

Carette sedan wipes out tin Penny Toy.

Clark friction auto.
Wood and metal. (1904)

Marx "Funny Cars". (1920's—30's)

Kingsbury
clockwork truck.
(1920's)

Bing and "Ebo"
autos wait for
mite size cars
to pass.
(1914—1930)

Merry Christmas

◆ For the very young, toys and Christmas are one and the same. Santa is still believable and we have yet to reach that age of disappointment when shirts and socks fill the gift boxes instead of those joyous old toys!

Stereo photo, circa 1895.

Christmas standards: Drum, Horn, Top and Game.

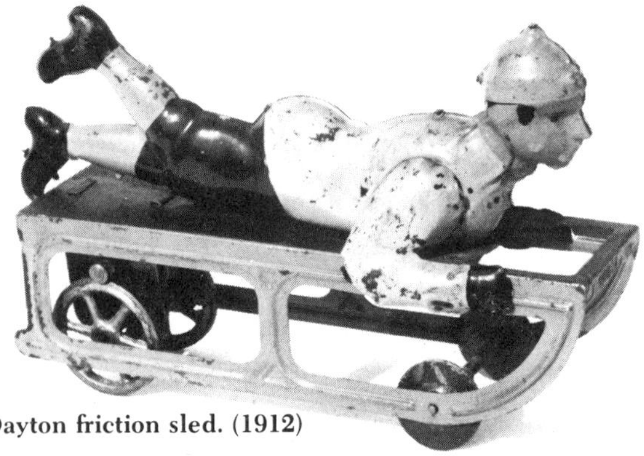

Dayton friction sled. (1912)

Hubley cast iron Santa and Sleigh. (1920)

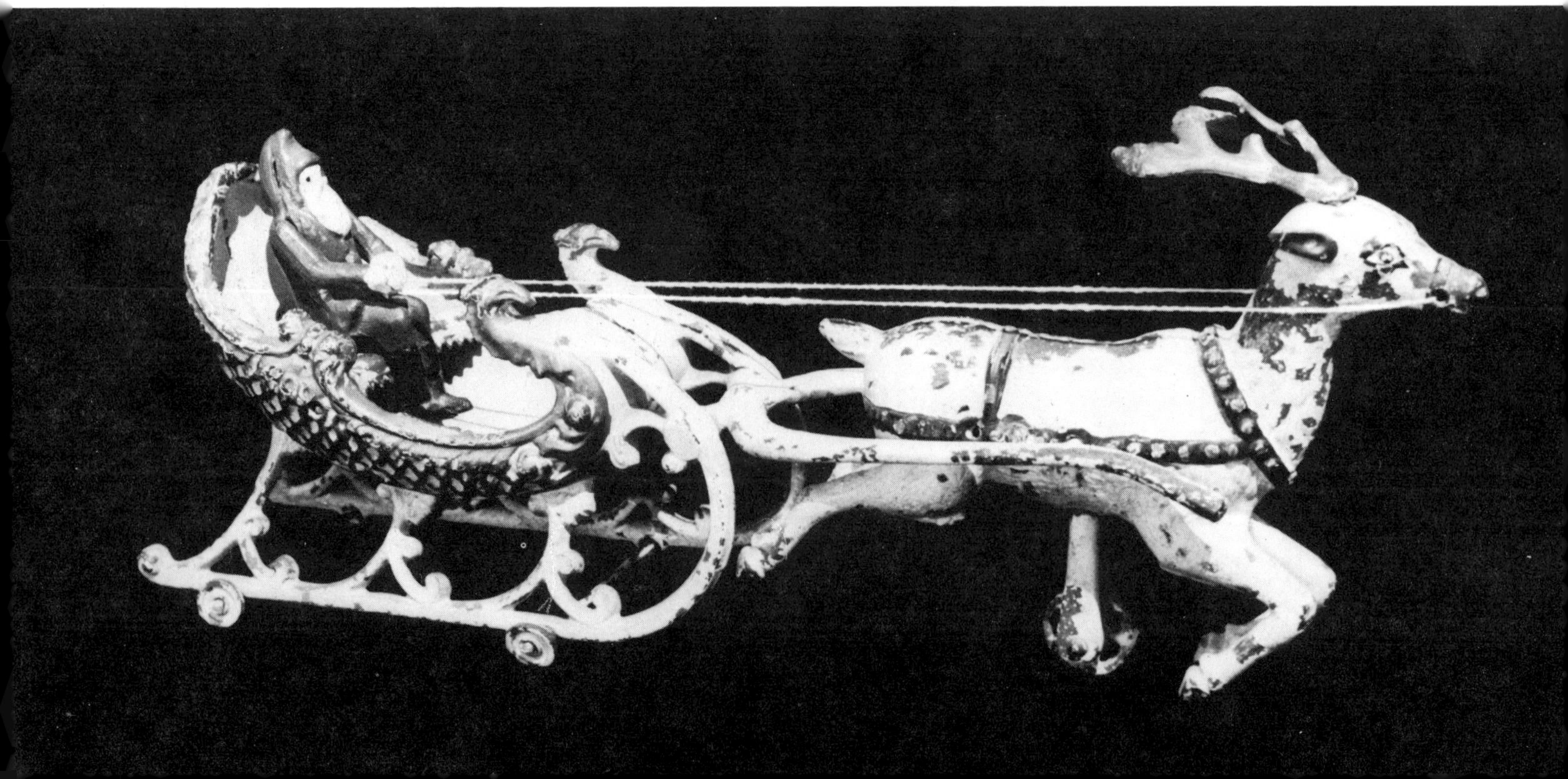